The Ladder of Faithfulness

D. Michael Henderson

Rafiki Books
450 Columbus Circle
Longwood, Florida 32750
www.rafikibooks.com

PRESS

Table of Contents

The Ladder of Faithfulness

At the end of his earthly ministry, Jesus commissioned his followers to "go into all the world and make disciples, . . .teaching them to do all I have commanded you to do." (Matthew 28:20) This assignment is a practical application of his overarching message: "Love God with all your heart, soul, mind, and strength and your neighbor as yourself." How do we best demonstrate our love for God? By making disciples, by giving personal spiritual attention to people, by "feeding the sheep" like the Good Shepherd did, by helping our friends follow Jesus. And how do we best put our love for our neighbor into action? By helping him follow Jesus.

Obviously, there are other ways to show our love for God and for our neighbor than by making disciples. However, the Great Commission is the primary consideration. All other means are subsidiary to the first. Jesus issued several commands which fall under the heading of "love God," like worship in spirit and truth, receive the Holy Spirit, pray to the Father, observe the sacraments, confess our sins, and follow him. And he gave several other approved means for showing love to our neighbors other than helping them become disciples: feeding those who are hungry, giving generously, taking the initiative in reconciliation, and helping free those who are oppressed.

According to both history and tradition, those first eleven disciples waited in Jerusalem for the Holy Spirit to come upon them, as Jesus had instructed, then set out to carry out the mission he had assigned them. The Book of Acts records the rapid expansion of the Church, as the original disciples made more disciples, and those new disciples clustered into fellowships throughout the Roman Empire. Today, twenty centuries later, that Church is still seeking to carry out the original commission of Jesus, although encumbered by the weight of human traditions.

The Church is constantly renewing itself by getting back to its initial purpose. At many stages along the time-line of the Church's history, sincere followers have sought to return to the original mission. Today, a resurgence of interest in disciple-making is underway. Across the globe, local congregations and individuals are asking themselves, "Are we really doing what Jesus told us to do? Are we actually making disciples?"

At the outset, it is important to define "What is a disciple?" And "What does it mean to make disciples?" The answer to that question will narrow the field of potential methods. A disciple is one who trusts Jesus enough to follow him, one step at a time, wherever he leads. That entails both faith (understanding what God wants and trusting him enough to act upon it) and grace (the dynamic power of God's love). Following Jesus is impossible by human effort; it can't be done. No one, by his own strength or cleverness, can live like Jesus commanded him to live and accomplish what Jesus said to accomplish. But grace enables even the simplest follower to stay on the path.

The articulation of what it means to "make disciples" is the watershed between the authentic gospel and lesser attempts. How did Jesus himself define the objective of making disciples? What did he say is God's ultimate inten-tion? There is clear evidence in scripture that the goal is not how many people can get tickets to heaven, but how many can be transformed into the likeness of Christ. His aim was not only to give them eternal life, but to shape their character after his own and to empower them to carry out the work he began in the world.

When Jesus prayed for his disciples, he asked that God would "sanctify them by the truth; your word is truth. As you sent me into the world, I have sent them into the world. For them I sanctify myself that they too may be sanctified." (John 17:17-19) The Apostle Peter reiterated this same theme as he urged his fellow Christians to a life of holiness, like God's holiness. (I Peter 1:15-16) John, the Beloved Disciple, affirmed the same purpose: that Jesus' disciples are to become like their teacher, made complete in the kind of love that Jesus himself demonstrated. (I John 3:2-3, and I John 4:16-18) The writer to the Hebrews underscored the same objective: that Christians should reflect God's holiness and be at peace with everyone. (Hebrews 12:14). And in every one of his letters, the Apostle Paul stated his mission as "urging you to live lives worthy of God, who calls you into his kingdom and glory." (I Thessalonians 2:12)

The term currently in vogue for this goal is "Christlikeness," and it is a good one. Christlikeness has both an inward focus and an outward expression. The inward goal is Christlike character, the fruit of the Spirit, maturity, full stature, living lives worthy of our calling as God's children, the mind of Christ, personal holiness. The external goal is that the believer will be equipped to do God's work in the world.

The Apostle Paul expressed this two-sided goal in his letter to young Timothy:

> "So that the man of God will be complete,
> thoroughly equipped for every good work."
> (II Timothy 3:17 King James Version)

9

God calls people not only to join his family, but to be workers in the family business. Jesus called this business "the Kingdom of God," extending God's authority over every aspect of human activity. His kingdom begins in the hearts of people and extends through them to the good they will do in society, transforming the world from within like yeast transforms bread dough.

A popular version of the gospel, which I call "Christianity Lite" defines "making disciples" only in terms of personal eternal salvation. It offers discipleship as an instantaneous transaction by which an individual may receive the gift of eternal life. "Just raise your hand, and your name will be written in the Lamb's Book of Life, never to be erased." The churches which subscribe to this doctrine are filled with baby Christians who have taken the first step in following Jesus, but have made little or no progress toward becoming like Christ in their character or engaged in his work.

Those "Christianity Lite" churches have a vast arsenal of tools to get people to acknowledge that Jesus is their ticket to heaven. A myriad of methods is available to enable people to "accept Christ," "get saved," "make a decision," "let Jesus come into your heart," and they have the numbers to prove that it works. "We showed a movie about Jesus to one billion people and half responded. Now they're bound for heaven."

An important question to ask is this: "Did Jesus make this kind of offer? Did he say to the crowd of 5,000, "Just fill out this card and you will be saved?" No, he said, "Take up a cross and follow me," and most of them went away.

Few churches practice the means to bring people to full maturity in Christ, to the character of Jesus and the ability to do his work in the world. Consequently, the methods for bringing people to full maturity in Christ are in short supply. Yet, certain secrets for making disciples can be gleaned from various groups and individuals who have been successful in this venture, all through the history of the Christian endeavor.

In every case the key is getting back to the Bible itself. How did Jesus make disciples? What can we learn from the models of Peter, James, Paul, Barnabas, and other biblical disciple-builders?

One core issue is whether the Bible is not only the message book, but also the methods manual for making disciples. It is becoming increasingly clear that the methods chosen to make disciples will not only determine the outcome of the process, but shape the doctrine of the Church as well. The choice of tools for producing followers of Jesus will pre-determine what kind of disciples will be formed.

There are many ways to visualize the process of progressing from raw unbelief and outright rebellion against God to full maturity in Christ, from doing what is disgusting in God's sight to what is good and right and constructive and Christlike. **I think of this continuum of spiritual growth as a ladder.** At the bottom is the pool of humanity in which I live and have friends: my neighborhood, my church, my school, my community, my city. At the top is Christlikeness: people who demonstrate the "mind of Christ" and do his work. How am I going to obey Jesus' command and do my part to bring people from this pool of humanity to spiritual maturity? What tools will I use? What methods? Who are my partners in this mission? What resources are available to me? Which people should I choose to start with, and how will I know when they are ready to move up to the next level, to take the next step?

After clarifying the goal ("bringing people to Christlikeness"), the next step is to identify the target group. How many people can I realistically expect to influence? Jesus spent three years with twelve followers, the last six months with three. Should we expect more? He healed many, and spoke to thousands, but whom did he choose to be his disciples? He chose those who were faithful. His public audience was anyone who would listen. His healing ministry was open to anyone who believed he could do it. But he limited his disciple-building ministry to those who were faithful, who were willing to follow him wherever he led and obey whatever he commanded. This is my central thesis: Jesus invested in the faithful ones. He filtered them out from the crowd and gave them special attention. He tailored his methods to their spiritual readiness—to whichever step they occupied on the ladder of spiritual growth.

Jesus illustrated the importance of faithfulness in his parables about stewards. (see Matthew 24:42-51 and 25:14-23) A steward is a manager whose responsibility is to accomplish his master's goals. The measure of the steward's work is his (or her) faithfulness, and the reward for faithful service at one level is additional responsibility on the next higher level. Jesus clearly expected that his disciples, not only the original twelve but all those who would follow after, to be faithful stewards in carrying out his mission.

Again, the Apostle Paul explained this process to Timothy:

"The things you have heard of me among many
witnesses, the same commit to faithful men who
will be able to teach others also." (II Timothy 2:2)

So, how was Timothy to determine which ones were faithful, and which were not? Not everyone who seems to be faithful will follow the process all the way to completion. On what basis did Jesus choose Judas, who proved not to be faithful? Only a cynic would conclude that Jesus deliberately chose someone to betray him. I believe Jesus chose Judas by the same criterion that he chose the other eleven: he appeared to be faithful. But at some point, "Satan entered his heart" and he abandoned Christ.

Paul and Barnabas faced a similar dilemma: Is John Mark a faithful worker or not? John Mark had moved up the ladder of discipleship to the point of risky and sacrificial service, but had not been willing to take the next step. Paul said, "I won't have a quitter on my team." Barnabas said, "I think he just needs more coaching." The two leaders went separate ways based on their estimate of John Mark's potential for serious discipleship. Apparently, Barnabas was right, for later on Paul wrote, "Bring John Mark with you, because he is a valuable man for the ministry." (II Timothy 4:11) It should be of some encouragement to modern-day disciple-builders that choosing faithful people is a subjective decision, and often mistaken.

A disciple progresses up the ladder of spiritual growth on the basis of faithfulness. Reliability at one level is a prerequisite for moving up to the next level. Not every person can be talented, intelligent, or gifted, but anyone can be faithful. Therefore, the ladder has open access.

The Ladder of Faithfulness
Christlikeness
(mature, equipped)

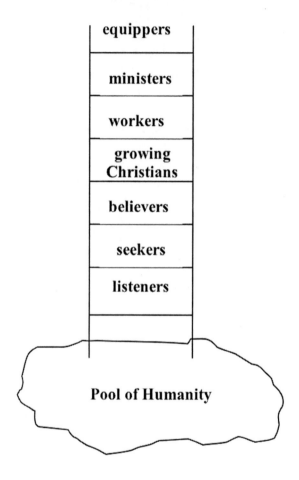

equippers

ministers

workers

growing
Christians

believers

seekers

listeners

Pool of Humanity

Let's examine the rungs on the ladder to Christlikeness: I'll start with the **seekers**, although there are some rungs below that level and several above. A seeker is someone who is willing (faithful) to take the first step in knowing and following Jesus: he or she has taken some initiative to examine the claims of Christ. Perhaps she is attending church services, or he is reading books about world religions. They are more than passive listeners: they are searching for the truth.

Jesus gave us the assurance that "everyone who is seeking the truth will recognize my voice." (John 18:37) That affirmation provides the confidence for those of us who want to make disciples to ask seekers to make the next step: believing enough in Jesus to trust their lives to him. Once that presentation has been made (or made many times) the seeker must make a choice: either to follow Jesus in faith or to turn away.

The responsibility of the disciple-maker is to identify those who are sincere seekers and to see that they have an opportunity to make the step from unbelief to faith, from going their own way to following Jesus. Part of that responsibility is warning the seeker about the consequences of ignoring or refusing the claims of Christ. Paul put it this way,

> "So naturally I proclaim Christ. I warn everyone I meet and teach everyone I can all that I know about him, so that, if possible, I may bring every man up to full maturity in Christ. That is what I am working at with all the strength God gives me." (Colossians 1:28-29, Phillips Translation)

The next rung on the ladder is **the believer**, the new Christian, the "babe in Christ," the convert. He or she has made a commitment to trust Jesus, not only for eternal salvation, but to follow him in faith. New believers have crossed the frontier from unbelief to faith and need to learn how to live in this new territory. They must be surrounded by the fellowship of other believers, affirmed and assured by the Word of God, and encouraged to trust God for the grace to grow in Christ.

The next step in the progression toward Christlikeness is spiritual growth. **Growing Christians**, like all growing organisms, need a steady intake of nutrients, a regular diet of nourishing spiritual "food." Nourishment starts with milk, then progresses to solid foods. The writer to the Hebrews uses the same metaphor: milk and meat. (I Corinthians 3:2, Hebrews 5:12)

Jesus promised that once we begin following him, he provides us with a personal guide, a mentor, an encourager, a teacher who will lead us in the path of discipleship. That teacher is his Holy Spirit, whose functions are to:

1. convict us of wrong behavior and attitudes
2. lead us into all truth
3. comfort us when we're sad
4. encourage us when we're down
5. show us the way
6. open scripture to our understanding

So, what does a growing Christian need? He/she needs to develop the skills, habits, disciplines, practices, and tools for living with the aid of the Holy Spirit.

John, one of Jesus' inner circle, addressed these growing Christians as "young men" in I John 2:14:

"I write to you, young men, because you are strong, and the word of God lives in you, and you have overcome the evil one."

So what do growing Christians need?

1. To develop spiritual strength
2. To build the word of God into their lives
3. To overcome the evil one (bad habits, wrong attitudes, fears, etc.)

Ideally, the next level of Christlikeness is **workers**—Christians who are serving in God's kingdom, whether among fellow Christians, or out in the community, or both. However, in many cases, these steps are out of order: new believers are given work assignments before they develop the "habits of holiness"—the disciplines of spiritual growth. This has at least three serious consequences:

1. They make a mess of their tasks because of their spiritual immaturity.
2. Their spiritual growth is dwarfed because their "busyness" with doing good takes up the time they should be developing spiritual strength.
3. They get into the habit of doing God's work in the power of the flesh, rather than in the power of the Holy Spirit.

Ministers are those who take responsibility for the spiritual welfare of other people. Timothy began at the bottom of the ladder as a timid teenage believer. By the time Paul wrote to the Philippians, he was able to say of Timothy: "I have no one else like him, who takes a genuine interest in your welfare." (Philippians 2:20-23) Timothy had become a minister.

The lady who opens her home to host a Bible study for her neighbors is a minister, the pastor who shepherds a flock of growing Christians is a minister, the Sunday School teacher who explains Bible stories to wiggling pre-schoolers is a minister. The key issue is not a matter of position or official recognition; it is a matter of the heart.

Ministers are spiritual mothers and fathers: they not only produce spiritual offspring, but they make sure those new Christians are nourished and protected from spiritual harm. The measure of the health of a church is not how many people attend its services, but how many become spiritual mothers and fathers. Too often churches are lulled into thinking they are successful because the numbers are increasing in various "silos": worship services, Sunday School, prayer meetings, or vacation Bible schools. What they should be measuring is how many people are making progress up the ladder of spiritual growth. Churches stagnate when their pastors must spend the majority of their time and energy working with people on the lower rungs of the ladder. When that work should be done by a growing corps of ministers.

Certain individuals at the highest level of Christlike maturity are given by God as gifts to the Church to shape its direction and to maintain Jesus' original mission. Their roles are described in several passages of scripture, but most succinctly in Paul's letter to the Ephesians:

> "It was he (Christ) who gave some to be apostles, some to be prophets, some to be evangelists, and some to be pastors and teachers, to prepare (equip) God's people for works of service, so that the body of Christ may be built up until we all reach unity in the faith and in the knowledge of the Son of God and become mature, attaining to the whole measure of the fullness of Christ." (Ephesians 4:11-13)

The specific responsibilities of apostles and prophets and evangelists and pastor/teachers may vary, but their function is the same: to equip believers for the work of ministry. For this reason, I lump them all together at the top of the ladder as **"equippers."** Notice also their assignment: to maintain unity in the Church and bring people to "the fullness of Christ." This is the basis for the wording of our mission statement: Making Christlike disciples. It is both a personal and corporate goal: not only must individuals seek to be like Jesus, but the whole Body must grow in relational likeness to him.

These "equippers" are charged with the task of directing the entire disciple-building process of the Church. Apostles are the pace-setters, the pioneers, who maintain the central mission of the Church. Prophets guard the heart of the Church from impurity and false motives, boldly calling the people of God to repentance and brokenness before God. Evangelists proclaim the gospel to unbelievers, and pastor/teachers present the Word of God in useful and helpful ways. Just as in the Book of Acts, these "equippers" constantly call the Church to "devote themselves to the apostles' teaching and to the fellowship, to the breaking of bread and to prayer." (Acts 2:42) They are the guardians of God's truth.

Some people who have looked at this "ladder of discipleship" have asked, "Where do leaders fit on this chart? We have invested heavily in 'leadership training' seminars and conferences to help our church be successful."

A key question to ask is, "Did Jesus train leaders?" No, he trained disciples. The only leaders mentioned in the New Testament are Caiaphas and Herod, the blind leaders of the blind (Matthew 15:14), and false teachers who lead silly women into lust and temptation (II Timothy 3:6). We already have a Leader; what we need are more diligent followers.

And what about learners? Shouldn't they also be on the ladder of spiritual growth? Yes, they are—at every level. Disciples are people who are learning to follow Jesus—at many different stages of development. As seekers, they are learning the claims of Christ; as new believers, they are learning what it means to be children of God; as growing Christians, they are learning the habits of holiness; as workers, they are learning the skills and information necessary to their callings; as ministers, they are learning the art of spiritual mentoring; as equippers, they are learning the "ways of God." No rung of the ladder is reserved for learners, since learning is the function of every stage of discipleship.

There is certainly a sense in which every Christian, at whatever level, needs to be a learner of God's Word. However, most churches depend too heavily on cognitive instruction and too little on the development of Christ-like attitudes, motives, ambitions, affections, and loyalties—issues of the heart. Information without application leads to spiritual self-deception—a false Christianity—as described by James:

> Do not merely listen to the word, and so deceive yourselves. Do what it says. Anyone who listens to the word but does not do what it says is like a man who looks at his face in a mirror and, after looking at himself, goes away and immediately forgets what he looks like. But the man who looks intently into the perfect law that gives freedom, and continues to do this, not forgetting what he has heard, but doing it—he will be blessed in what he does." (James 1:22-25)

There are two rungs on the ladder below seekers. One is those people out there in the community who have no particular interest in religion, but are at least open to **listen** to what Christians around them have to say.

Also, there is **the whole community** in which we live, made up of every shade of spiritual interest. We do have an obligation to them, and we need to treat them as an entirely separate category.

Appropriate Methods

The modern church has at its disposal a vast array of methods and materials for ministering to people, far more than Jesus had when he established the original model. However, the question must always be asked, "Are the methods we are currently using actually producing disciples?" If not, why should we continue using those tools? Let's examine some of the tools in our modern-day toolbox for making disciples:

Tools:

Sunday school	Conversations	Seminaries
Student ministries	Interpretive dance	Books
Testimonies	Prayer	City-wide crusades
Scripture memory	Sermons	Church buildings
Tent meetings	Retreats	Pastors
Camp meetings	Sunday services	Television
Christian colleges	Films	programs
Tracts	Websites	Hymnbooks
Home groups	Social networks	Private Schools
Mission trips	Mentoring	Drama

Retreats	Daily devotionals	Chat rooms
Sports teams	Revival meetings	(many more)
Counseling	Denominations	
Devotional classics	Christian music	

Whenever we choose a particular method, we should always ask:

1. Is this one of the methods used by Jesus or the early Christians to make disciples? If not, what cautions do we need to take?
2. Does this tool actually bring people closer to the goal of becoming a mature disciple of Jesus, "fully equipped for every good work?"
3. Is it culturally appropriate?
4. What are the possible unintended consequences?
5. Will we be able to lay it down once we're finished with it? Or will it become an entrenched institution?
6. How will it affect our doctrine?

Lets' expand on some of these questions:

1. The foundational question is: What methods did Jesus use to make disciples? And, as the early Christians gathered into churches, what additional tools did they employ? (It would be an interesting study to look back through history and gauge the effect(s) which any particular new method—like church buildings in the fourth century or city-wide crusades in the 19th—had on the church and its understanding of the gospel.)

From the outset, Jesus made it clear that being a disciple entailed influencing other people. "Follow me, and I will make you fishers of men." (Matthew 4:19, Mark 1:17) Jesus called the Twelve "that they might be with him and that he might send them out to preach. . ." (Mark 3:14) Everything the disciples learned from Jesus was couched in the expectation that those principles and practices would be used by them to train future disciples. Genuine discipleship was not, and should not be, a self-focused exercise. It must always entail equipping to serve others.

The context of Jesus' disciple-training program was everyday life: walking along the road, eating in the homes of friends, talking to people in the marketplace, or worshipping in the synagogue. It is reminiscent of the pattern of instruction given to the children of Israel in Deuteronomy 6:

Hear, O Israel: The Lord our God, the Lord is one. Love the Lord your God with all your heart and with all your soul and with all your strength. These commandments that I give you today are to be upon your hearts. Impress them on your children. Talk about them when you sit at home and when you walk along the road, when you lie down and when you get up. (Deuteronomy 6:5-7)

Jesus chose illustrations from daily life: bread, water, light, work, neighbors, animals, trees, etc. He used parables and riddles to unfold profound truths and apply them to the understanding of God's kingdom.

In educational circles, this is called non-formal education. Formal education has a pre-set scope and sequence; it has clearly defined outcomes. Informal education is a learning experience with no prior goal or plan—it just happens, like putting your hand on a hot stove and learning not to do that again. Non-formal instruction has a clear-cut goal, but no particular sequence of lessons or topics. Issues are addressed as life-situations require them. In Jesus' instructional method, the goal was always clear: to become like the Master, to do as he did, to think as he thought, to speak as he spoke, and to live as he lived. "I AM the way, the truth, and the life," he said.

The "backbone" of Jesus instructional system was simply "Follow me!" "Do as I do." "Trust me enough to imitate my example." Jesus didn't teach them the plan of salvation; he was the Plan. He didn't explain the Word of God; he was the Word. He did not ask his disciples for mindless submission, because he walked with them every step of their spiritual journey.

The Apostle Paul built his instructional system on this same pattern, with the clear disclaimer that he was not the ultimate leader. "Follow me as I follow Christ," he said. (I Corinthians 11:1) He praised the Thessalonian church, (the only church called a model in scripture) because they imitated what he had modeled for them. (I Thessalonians 1:6)

The simplest definition of "making disciples" is "teaching people to follow Jesus." He set the curriculum for that process in the Great Commission, when he said, "teaching them to obey all I have commanded you." (Matthew 28:20)

Another foundational principle of Jesus' model is the disciple-making relationship: personal friendship. He clearly defined this in John 15:13-15:

> Greater love has no one than this, that he lay down his life for his **friends**. You are my **friends** if you do what I command. I no longer call you servants, because a servant does not know his master's business. Instead, I have called you **friends**, for everything that I learned from my Father I have made known to you.

The difference between friends and servants, as Jesus explained, is that friends share a common "business" and love each other enough to lay down their lives for each other.

Servants do what they're told; friends work together on a shared mission.

So, the basic definition of making disciples can be clarified one step further: "helping our friends follow Jesus."

Jesus' Methods

Let's select from the toolbox those tools which Jesus himself used.

A. Large gatherings.

To those who were willing to listen, Jesus explained the principles of God's kingdom in contrast to both the ways of the world and of traditional religion. He spoke to people wherever they gathered: in the temple courts, in the synagogues, on hillsides, or in the marketplace. It is important to note that in every case the audience came expecting to hear something religious. They were not tricked into listening to Jesus; they came willingly, even though they may have been skeptical or critical (like the Pharisees). He did not usurp other people's gatherings, like displaying a "John 3:16" banner at sports events. The people chose to hear what he had to say; whether they accepted it or not was up to them.

B. Personal conversations

Jesus had personal, direct, open conversations with individual people at every level of discipleship: serious followers (Peter, James, John), willing hearers (the woman at the well of Samaria), as-yet-unconvinced seekers (Nicodemus), and hostile critics (Pilate, the Pharisees). In each case, he asked probing questions, seeking to get down to base reality—

issues of the heart. And, often, he used shocking statements to drive his point home: "You must be born again!" "Let him who is without sin cast the first stone."

One of Jesus' most common uses of personal conversation was to follow up his public teaching. To those who kept asking, "What do these things mean?" Jesus gave personal and intense attention. This is a good model for modern-day disciple-builders to emulate, as we will discuss later.

C. Gatherings in homes

Jesus set an example for his disciples by doing much of his teaching in family homes. He chose an instructional environment which is appropriate for every culture in every period of history. The home atmosphere allowed for discussion and feedback. He was able to handle much more personal and emotional issues in a family setting, like the death of a family member (Lazarus), extravagant worship (the woman who poured oil on his feet), and betrayal (Judas). He selected Zacchaeus from the crowd and invited himself to Zacchaeus' home for dinner. Perhaps he even allowed the roof in his own house to be destroyed so a lame man could be healed. (Mark 2:1-12)

Jesus often taught in the home of Lazarus, Mary, and Martha. In Simon Peter's home, he healed Simon's mother-in-law; in Matthew's home he entertained tax collectors; in the home of Jairus, he healed the man's daughter; in a home in Capernaum he took a child on his lap to illustrate the kingdom; in a home in Tyre/Sidon he healed the Syrophoenician woman; and in a home in Jerulsalem he ate the Last Supper with his disciples.

The early church met in homes. The Book of Acts records that "they broke bread together in their homes," and "they were preaching and teaching in every home." There are specific references in the New Testament to meetings in the homes of Cornelius, Mary, the Phillippian jailer, Jason,

Aquila and Priscilla, Crispus, Phillip, Stephanus, Nympha, Philemon, and Onesiphorus.

D. Prayer

The only thing his disciples asked Jesus to teach them was how to pray. They had witnessed his own practice of prayer. He prayed with them and for them. One of his most powerful tools for personal growth was visualizing spiritual progress for them in prayer. He prayed that:

> "they may have the full measure of my joy within them"
> "they would be protected from the evil one."
> "they all may be one" (John 17)

The Apostle Paul used prayer as a primary tool for helping the members of his team to take the next steps. "I pray for you that. . ."

- You may be active in sharing your faith (Philemon 1:6)
- You may be rooted and established in love (Ephesians 3:16)
- The eyes of your heart may be enlightened (Ephesians 1:18)
- Your love may abound more and more in knowledge and depth of insight (Philippians 1:9)

E. Cross-cultural journeys

In a first-century prototype of mission trips, Jesus took his disciples on ministry sorties through alien territory: Samaria, Judea, and Jerusalem. The twelve (except for Judas) were rustic Galileans; they spoke with rural accent. They experienced just as much culture shock traveling through Samaria as today's short-term mission-trippers experience in the slums of Nairobi or the high-rise buildings of Hong Kong. The primary subject matter of those training missions was the universality of God's kingdom. Those experiences forced the disciples to think of God's work beyond the boundaries of their own provincial thinking.

Paul expanded the mission journey model with wide-ranging trips into the territories of the Gentiles. This is where he trained his workers.

F. Doing good

The public "walkabout" style of Jesus teaching was nearly always in the context of doing good, meeting the practical needs of people he met along the way. He healed the sick, fed the hungry, and cast demons out of those who were possessed. These were not miracles-on-demand shows, as popularized by T.V. evangelists, but simply meeting the real needs of people in the power of the Holy Spirit.

G. Giving new meaning to traditional religious events

Jesus did not shun the religious ceremonies of his people; he filled the empty shells with new meaning. He observed the Passover, but introduced a new covenant. He visited the temple, but prophesied his own resurrection. He submitted to baptism, but promised a baptism with God's Spirit. He practiced the common tradition of washing the feet of guests, but he gave it new meaning.

At least on one occasion (in Athens, as reported in Acts 17:23), the Apostle Paul used the religions of the Gentiles as a starting point for a presentation of the gospel. In every newly-formed congregation, his colleagues were forced to grapple with the cultural questions which arose as the gospel of the kingdom clashed with other religions and traditions. The purpose of those trips was not only to plant the flag of the Jerusalem/Antioch church in new territories, but to equip cross-cultural workers.

The critical questions are these: Are these the methods we are using for making disciples today? Are they the primary tools, or add-ons to the preferred methods of "doing church?" And, do we really need any other tools than those Jesus used?

Could we make disciples in the 21st century without church buildings, television shows, city-wide crusades, websites, counseling centers, Christian day schools, Sunday Schools, and bowling leagues? Certainly! It doesn't mean we shouldn't use those tools, but they must not usurp the role of the primary methods Jesus taught us. Every other technique than Jesus' own should include warning labels: "Caution! This method could be dangerous or fatal to your spiritual health!"

We need to do a deep study of "the ways of God." The Psalmist said, "He made known his ways to Moses, his deeds to the people of Israel." (Psalm 103:7) Most of the Israelites simply observed the mighty acts of God; they saw what he did. But Moses learned the "why?" and the "how?" of God's interaction with his people. In the New Testament sermon against the sin of unbelief (Hebrews 3 and 4), the expositor of Psalm 95 explains that the Israelites were condemned to wandering in the desert because "their hearts were not right and they did not understand the ways of God." The "ways of God" are the means, the methods, by which God does things. Most people are satisfied to witness the mighty acts of God, but true disciples seek to understand his ways. They are as concerned with "how?" as "what?" This is a key issue for mission executives, denominational leaders, and church strategists.

I was recently asked by a church executive, "What do you think of our denomination?"

I said, politely, "Do you remember the story of David taking the ark of the covenant up to Jerusalem from Baalah in Judah? (II Samuel 6) He put it on a cart drawn by oxen;

when it tipped over, his friend Uzzah reached up to steady it and was struck down dead. David was deeply grieved, and the ark stayed there for quite a while. The whole project was delayed and the joy of its accomplishment marred by the death of Uzzah.

So, where did David get the idea of carrying the ark on a wagon? He got it from the Philistines. God had given specific instructions in Deuteronomy about how the ark should be carried so this very thing would not happen. When it finally got to Jerusalem, the whole project was tainted by the use of improper methods.

That's a picture of your denomination: God's dear people, doing what they believe to be God's will, but they are borrowing their methods from the Philistines. The end result is a lot of unnecessary anguish and a diminished end result."

Two key questions I ask when any method is under consideration: will this work in Somalia, and can a mentally retarded person use this method? If not, the method probably doesn't have universal application. Not long ago, I took a tour of a theological seminary which has co-opted the term "discipleship." They want to believe they are training people to make disciples. They showed me with great pride their new $900,000 pipe organ and expected me to be overwhelmed. I asked two questions which sounded foolish to them: will this work in Somalia, and can a mentally retarded person participate in this?

McDonalds Corporation does a much better job answering the second question than the church. Yes, mentally handicapped people can attend church services, if they're quiet and don't disrupt what's going on. But at McDonalds, they can have a real job, play an important role in service to the customer, and get paid for it!

It is fascinating to realize that the methods Jesus used to make disciples transcend culture and time. His instructional tools are as relevant to making disciples among the pygmies in the rain forests of Cameroun as they are to making disciples in the corporate boardrooms of New York or the universities in South Africa. One-to-one conversations about spiritual growth worked in the first century, John Wesley found them useful in the 18th century, and they are still the most effective tool for helping people grow. As Wesley said, "I can see more spiritual growth in one hour of 'close conversation' than in ten years of preaching."

2. Will we be able to lay them down?

My father had a favorite story about church activities which he learned from his father: An enormous herd of sheep was moving down a country road, led by a wise old ram. As the lead sheep approached an intersection, a young lady on a bicycle was approaching on the cross road. The old ram realized that if she had to wait for all those sheep to cross, she would be delayed for hours. The old ram knew he couldn't stop, because of all the sheep pushing from behind. Being the gentleman that he was, he came up with a creative solution: he jumped high in the air, giving her room to pass safely under and continue on her way. Late that night, as the young lady was safely at home and having supper, the sheep were still jumping over the same intersection, but no one knew why. What had started out as a creative idea turned into a senseless institution.

3. How will this method shape our doctrine?

My personal spiritual roots are in what is known as "the holiness movement." This distinct branch of the church grew out of a unique American method: the camp meeting. These annual gatherings sprang up on the American frontier in the mid-1800's, held during the lull in the farming season—between the last cultivation and harvest, usually late July or

August. This was a gathering for serious believers, not for seekers or the mildly interested.

For ten days or two weeks, eloquent and passionate preachers called already-committed Christians to a deeper walk with Christ. Their stock-in-trade was an "experience" which rolled together several biblical themes—all legitimate scriptural emphases: the sanctifying ministry of the Holy Spirit, baptism in the Holy Spirit, personal holiness, empowerment for service, and the Spirit-controlled life. Just like on the day of Pentecost, when the Holy Spirit came upon the assembled believers, camp meeting attendees were encouraged to seek that experience which would lift their spiritual existence to a higher level. Thus, they called themselves "Pentecostals."

Once the camp meeting (and its indoor cousin, the revival meeting) became an accepted method, the method began shaping the theology of its practitioners. How would they define this experience born of the camp meeting? How would it be woven into the fabric of orthodox doctrine? It came to be called "the second work of grace," as distinguished from the initial experience of salvation by grace through faith. And why did believers need the "second work" offered by the camp meetings? Salvation brought forgiveness from actual sins; the second experience needed to deal with something. The idea emerged that sanctification dealt with the guilt associated with Augustine's concept called "original sin." That is, since Adam sinned, his guilt is somehow passed on to all his progeny, and that guilt must somehow be managed. The doctrine which grew out of the camp meeting experience was defined as eradicating or suppressing the effects of original sin.

This was a new concept in Christian theology. John Wesley, the theological forefather of the holiness movement, taught that believers could arrive at a state of "perfect love," in which their motives were pure and their behavior pleasing to God. He called this "scriptural holiness," which had both personal and social implications. However, his doctrine was shaped by an entirely different set of instructional tools. His methods (for which he was labeled a "Methodist") were an interlocking hierarchy of small and intimate fellowships. The "Methodist theology" which ensued was shaped by that environment and those distinct instructional tools.

The camp meeting, then, shaped the doctrine of the holiness movement. As Marshall McLuhan aptly observed, "The medium is the message." If not an entirely adequate explanation, at least it is accurate to say that the medium shapes the message.

In 1904, the Pentecostal/holiness movement took a surprising turn: a group of students at a Bible college in Topeka, Kansas, added a new dimension to the "second work of grace." They asked, "But how do you KNOW that you have been baptized in the Holy Spirit, sanctified, and made holy?" They came to the conclusion that "the initial evidence of the baptism of the Holy Spirit is speaking in tongues," as occurred on the Day of Pentecost. They sought such evidence, and within a week they began to experience the phenomenon of speaking in tongues. The practice spread like wildfire. With the onset of the Azusa Street Revival in California, which popularized the new interpretation of the baptism with the Holy Spirit, a whole new movement was born. These were the true Pentecostals, and they could prove it: they spoke in tongues.

The camp meeting people were in a quandary: they had been upstaged by upstarts. Who were these Johnny-come-latelys to usurp their distinctive niche in the Christian world? Reluctantly, and over a period of several years, the holiness movement let the new Pentecostals have the name. They still held camp meetings and revivals, but refocused their energies into a new methodology: holiness denominations. Once again, the method bent the message. The new denominations with their publishing houses, their colleges and seminaries, and their mission agencies adapted the message of holiness to fit their organizational needs. What had begun in the camp meetings as a message about personal piety gradually morphed into corporate identities. "Holiness" was no longer a noun; it became an adjective—"We are holiness people." Or even, "We are holiness."

The Pentecostals experienced their own metamorphosis, emerging from their blue-collar and African-American cocoon to reappear in middle-class and upwardly-mobile form. They, too, consolidated their numerical gains into Pentecostal denominations, again with colleges, publishing houses, seminaries, and mission agencies. Those are still with us, as are the holiness denominations, but with dwindling numbers and social significance.

However, two new methods took the Pentecostal message in two entirely new directions: prayer fellowships in mainline churches and television.

Beginning in the early 1960's, renewal movements sprang up within traditional non-Pentecostal denominations, like the Episcopalians, Methodists, and Presbyterians. Some people within those churches grew dissatisfied with dry liturgy, anemic preaching, and social activism. They wanted more. The method they chose was prayer fellowships—small renewal groups meeting in homes to seek a more intimate relationship with Christ. They prayed with fervor, and some spoke in tongues as an expression of their worship and praise. The doctrine of this new charismatic movement was shaped by its method: prayer fellowships. Unlike their Pentecostal brethren, they did not interpret the experience of speaking in tongues as the initial evidence of being baptized in the Spirit. Instead, it was a "prayer language" and not indicative of anything other than a desire to speak to God more intimately.

Television took Pentecostalism in a different direction, dictated by the costs of the medium itself. The stock-in-trade of the television evangelist was neither the baptism of the Holy Spirit as in earlier Pentecostalism, nor a prayer language as in the charismatic movement, nor a sanctification experience as offered by the holiness movement. It was personal success, prosperity, positive thinking, and the realization of personal potential. The "Prosperity Gospel" was not only birthed by the financial requirements of an expensive medium; it was shaped by the nature of the method itself.

Every choice of a method has consequences for the message it purports to convey. Those unintended consequences must be critically considered when organizations or individuals choose a medium to communicate their message. The intent of this essay is not a cynical critique of the roots of American movements; it is rather an appeal to trust the scriptures as not only our message book, but our method book. What means did Jesus use to make disciples? And what were the means by which the early church communicated the message to the pagan world?

Methods For Each
Level of Readiness

One of the major instructional blunders of the modern church is the assumption that one (or two or three) public gathering each week can or will serve growing Christians at all levels. This one-size-fits-all formula is followed throughout the world in evangelical churches. There are slight variations from one church to another, but essentially the same, as though it were handed down from apostles:

Call to Worship (or "Good Morning" or "Howdy")
Announcements (even though they are printed in
the bulletin)
Three songs out of the hymnal (congregation seated,
one hand may be raised)
Prayer (by ordained clergy only)
Offering (either bags or plates), accompanied by
organ music
Worship songs (standing the whole time, both hands
may be raised)
Scripture reading
Special music (choir, ensemble, or solo)
Sermon
Invitation song
Benediction

Churches advertise themselves as "contemporary" if they juggle some of the components around or add drums and projected images during the "worship time," but the formula stays the same and the underlying assumptions are not challenged. Nobody seems to question the premise that this is the appropriate way to bring people from unbelief to Christlikeness.

So, how did the evangelical (Protestant) church arrive at this formula? How did it choose this method of "making disciples," since it was clearly not the practice of the early church? In a very brief summary, the informal gatherings of the early church gradually crystallized into a set pattern of worship centered around the two sacraments of the Lord's Supper and baptism. The Lord's Supper became a formalized ceremony within a few generations of Jesus' death, burial, and resurrection. For the first three centuries or so, the communion meal was observed in homes where the church gathered. But after the fourth century, the practice was restricted to consecrated buildings: basilicas, cathedrals, and other buildings set aside solely for worship.

As Christianity moved toward becoming the official religion of the Roman Empire (which it did formally in 380 A.D. when Theodosius was Emperor), the ritual of observing the Lord's Supper was institutionalized as The Mass, or Missa. Its form was established on two questionable doctrines, which I call "literalizations" of two sets of Jesus' statements:

1. When Jesus said, "This is my body,… this is my blood," the Roman Church came to believe he meant that the physical bread and wine became his actual body and blood. This was the basis for establishing the ritual of communion as a reenactment of the crucifixion of Jesus, which was done every week by a consecrated priest.

2. Jesus statement that "upon this rock I will build my church" was literalized to mean that Simon Peter was set apart to be the official head of the church, and all who were consecrated by him would be priests. Only those ordained directly by Peter (in apostolic succession from then on) were qualified to conduct the mass. The sacred rite (the mass) included elements of Jewish synagogue prayers in the ritual, like scripture readings, psalm-singing, and moral instruction, but the core of the mass was the transformation of the bread and wine into Jesus' physical body and blood through a formula of "words of institution."

Since the mass was only for believers, the church was divided into two categories: those who had been baptized and *catechumens,* or those who were preparing for baptism. Latin was the language of the Roman Empire, so the mass was presented only in Latin (by the edict of the Pope), and it remained so until the liturgy of the mass was opened to other languages in the mid-20th century.

Also in the fourth century, as Christianity became the state church, other accoutrements were added to the mass, like incense, bells, chants, icons, relics, and elaborate garments. The essential elements of the mass have remained unchanged from the time of the Roman Empire until the present.

The history and doctrine of the mass is of little significance to those who have grown up in the Protestant tradition, following the lead of the 16th century reformers like Martin Luther, Martin Bucer, Ulrich Zwingli, John Calvin, and others. However, the Protestant Reformation challenged only the doctrine of the Catholic Church, not the underlying methodology. The practice remains the same: a weekly ceremony officiated by an ordained priest.

My father was a Protestant priest. During his lifetime of ministry, he served nine different parishes in Illinois and

Missouri. He performed the religious duties of a priest—baptize infants, perform weddings, bury the dead, conduct weekly worship ceremonies, pray for the sick and dying, and serve as personal chaplain to the members of the congregation. He would have been shocked by any suggestion that he was performing the same rites as a Roman Catholic priest, but his duties were the same: a consecrated elite conducting the religious ceremonies of a congregation. Only the theology was different.

My father was an extremely diligent priest. He worked hard on his sermons, called on his congregants regularly, prayed earnestly for his parishioners, and maintained an orderly parish. Wherever he was assigned by the bishop, the church grew and prospered. Every time he left, that same congregation declined. He did not serve the church poorly; the church served him poorly by placing him in a role which was not effective in making disciples.

The time has come for a new model. The formula handed down through the Roman Catholic Church and evangelical Protestantism is not working. It is not reaching the unchurched, it is not serving the needs of the community, it is not even reaching its own children. It is dying. Most important of all, it is not making disciples. It is not enabling people to become like Jesus and do his work in the world. The thesis of this study is that every level of spiritual maturity demands a different instructional approach. There is no "one-size-fits-all" formula which will address all levels at once.

I do not claim to have all the answers when it comes to making disciples. I do not have a magic formula, nor would I share it if I had one. I'm simply putting forth the challenge to accept a new platform on which to build a ministry which successfully carries out Jesus' commands: love God, love your neighbor, and make disciples. I am suggesting that the central mission of the church is an instructional task (to make disciples), not a weekly enactment of a religious ceremony. I will offer some suggestions about what kinds of instructional tools are appropriate for each level of spiritual growth, but I will leave it to others to fill up the nearly-empty toolbox with methods which have proven effective.

Seekers

Let's start again with the seekers: what methods are appropriate to bring them to faith in Christ? Remember: a seeker is someone who has already taken a step toward belief: attended a church service, read an intriguing book, heard the witness of a Christian friend, taken a class on world religions, or sat in on a city-wide evangelistic crusade. Unknowingly, he or she has responded to the prompting of the Holy Spirit to take a step toward faith in Jesus. Now, what does that person need in order to move from unbelief to faith?

The foundational need of a seeker is to see compelling evidence that following Jesus is the way to know God. He or she needs to witness changed lives and a community which reflects the love of Christ. Yes, the seeker needs to hear a clear presentation of Jesus' claims and his call upon his or her life. She needs to know who Jesus is, what he offers her, and what he asks of her. He needs to come to the point of believing that Jesus is in fact the Son of God, the savior of those who follow him. However, Jesus himself gave his followers the prescribed, universal method for calling people to himself: "You shall be my witnesses, in Jerusalem, and Judea, and Samaria and to the uttermost parts of the earth." This is how seekers become believers.

At the outset, this kind of trust in Christ entails the abandonment of any attempts to save oneself, a regret or remorse for having offended or neglected God, and a willingness to follow Jesus wherever he leads. "Believing" may happen in a moment; it may take months or years. Whatever the time frame, believing is crossing the frontier from unbelief to faith.

John Wesley, the 18th century Anglican preacher, had a successful method for bringing seekers to salvation. He called it "the class meeting." Whenever he would preach to large crowds of people, usually in open fields or marketplaces, he would invite those who were serious about seeking God to join a small group called a "class meeting." The only requirement was "a desire to flee the wrath to come." Every week, the members of a class met with a group of other Christians and answered a set of questions about their spiritual condition. They were encouraged to be honest and forthright, even if they were not able to claim "assurance of salvation." In a loving, supportive fellowship, they found the security to voice their doubts, admit their sins and weaknesses, and examine their own motives. In return, they were provided the nurture of a group of ordinary believers (no clergy) and the insights of others who had made the same journey. Best of all, seekers were able to witness the transforming power of the gospel. This was not an information meeting: there were no sermons, lectures, teachings, or even Bible readings. It was just a "means of grace" by which a seeker could be ushered into the family of God by fellow strugglers.

There was a fellow named Bob in some of my graduate courses at the university. He was a socially inept fellow, politely avoided by most of the other students because of his inappropriate remarks and untidy appearance. I tried to be friendly toward Bob, but I wasn't hoping he'd be my next best friend.

One day, just before Thanksgiving break, Bob approached me in the reading room. "Are you a priest?" he asked. "You seem to be religious."

"Well, something like that," I hedged.

"I'm quite interested in religion, and I'd like to talk with you about Christianity," he said.

Wow! Here's a seeker! What an opportunity! But I dropped the ball: "Bob, I'm getting ready for exams right now. Could we talk after we get back from break?"

When I bumped into Bob in the reading room after break, his face broke into a grin. "Guess what?" he said. "I've been converted!"

"Terrific, Bob! Tell me about it."

"I've become a Mormon!"

I tried to hide my dismay. "Swell, Bob, that's. . .really something. Tell me more."

"Well," he said, "I went to visit my cousin in Colorado, and she told me how she has become a Mormon. She was really excited about it, and I was happy for her. She tried to tell me all about Mormonism, but couldn't answer all my questions, so she asked if I would meet with some men from her church. Two guys came over to her house, every night for most of a week, and explained how my background as a Catholic was the perfect foundation for becoming a good Mormon. They gave me lots of information about the church and its teachings, and they brought stuff for me to read— when I have time. And they told me what I would need to do to become a leader in the church. That's a long way off, but I'm excited about starting."

"When I got back to Bloomington, it was 1:00 in the morning, but there were two brothers here to meet me and take me back to my apartment. They told me all about the student fellowship here, and they gave me a card." He pulled out his wallet and fished out a printed card. "This is the phone number I can call any time, day or night, if I have questions or need something—anything. They'll come to me wherever I am and help me." He smiled. "I feel like I have a whole new family."

I groaned. I felt guilty about my own negligence and frustrated that the evangelical church is letting the Mormons beat us at our own game.

The Mormons are growing rapidly because their methods are more biblical than ours. We call ourselves "Bible-believing Christians," but that's only half true: we believe the message of the Bible, but we don't practice the methods Jesus modeled. Here are some things the Mormons do which are more biblical than our evangelical model:

1. Every Mormon is a witness. They tell people about their experience in the church. This is what Jesus said should happen when the Holy Spirit comes: "You shall be my witnesses. . ."

2. Every Mormon is expected to be a missionary. Young Mormons commit two years of their lives to missionary training and on-the-job experience. This is not perceived as something they will do and "get it over with." No, the two years of missionary service is preparation for an entire life of outreach, service, witness, and evangelism.

3. They meet people in their homes. They don't call non-Mormons to public meetings. Here's an interesting statistic: Mormon missionaries going door-to-door report less than one convert for every thousand homes on whose doors they knock. However, when presentations are made in the home of a Mormon friend or relative, the conversion rate is more than 50%! Just like Jesus did!

4. In every local "ward," there are trained evangelists who can be called upon at any time to make a presentation for Mormonism. They're good at it. They receive

special training. These are not professional revivalists who travel around the country giving speeches in churches; these are local Mormons who are evangelizing local prospects. This is the Ephesians 4 pattern of the early church: apostles, evangelists, prophets, pastors/teachers.

5. From the very outset, a "ladder" of spiritual development is presented: a seeker is presented a picture of what he or she could become by faithful participation in the Mormon community, and it is a compelling motivator. Jesus did this. "Follow me, and I'll make you fishers of men."

6. The invitation to become a Mormon is not based on getting rid of guilt, but on gaining an abundant life. It is not a guilt management system. The focus is not on past sins, but on future fulfillment—not future fulfillment in eternity, but right now. This was Jesus' message: "The kingdom of heaven has come; it's right here, right now."

At the very time when most evangelical denominations are declining, and many churches are struggling to keep their doors open, Mormonism is growing at the rate of 52% per decade! Why? Because they are doing what Jesus told his disciples to do: they are making disciples, not converts.

One of my former students phoned to ask me to pray for an event he was conducting. "We're having evangelistic services at our church, and I'd like you to pray with us that people will be converted."

"Absolutely not!" I replied.

There was a long silence on the phone. Then he asked, "Why not?"

"First of all," I said, "it's highly unlikely that any unbeliever is going to wander into your church to hear an evangelist preach. Most of the people who will attend are your own faithful few. Second, you have no plan, no mechanism in place, to follow up those who might make a decision. Third, you aren't bringing the people in your church who are already believers to full maturity, to productive ministry, to personal growth."

Most evangelical churches base their appeal to seekers on one of two faulty assumptions:

1. That a seeker will be convinced by a rational argument.
2. That he or she is primarily concerned with the guilt of sin.

Yes, those are two legitimate issues which must be addressed. But, no, those appeals are not the basis on which most seekers make a decision to become Christians. Rather, as researchers are discovering, modern American seekers tend to make a commitment to join and stay in a Christian fellowship because they want to participate in the way of life exemplified by people they know and trust and admire.

When the appeal is made by a stranger who has no roots in the community, conversion is seen as a transaction which takes place in heaven, not as a here-and-now transformation which incorporates a former non-believer into the local branch of the universal family of God. It is a package deal which can be completed in one church service, or series of services, a response to an emotional sermon. When Jesus called his disciples, they were already part of a relational network on the shores of Lake Galilee. When Peter presented the gospel to Cornelius, a Roman centurion who was a sincere seeker, his whole household was converted.

A seeker needs to hear Jesus' call to acknowledge that the kingdom of God has come through his own cosmic intervention and join that kingdom by faith in him. He or she, the seeker, needs to hear that message in the context of an established fellowship of local Christians, the on-site representatives of God's kingdom who are able to nurture that newborn believer in his or her newfound faith.

I once participated in a city-wide "evangelistic campaign" conducted by telephone. Hundreds of volunteers, like me, went down through the phone book and "presented the gospel" to anyone who would listen to the full script. Thousands of "decisions" were reported, and their names were given to local churches to follow up. However, one year later a research team surveyed the churches in our city and could not find one person who had joined a church as a result of that effort. Is that because the telephone is not an appropriate method for talking to people about joining God's kingdom? No, it is simply evidence that appealing to seekers outside the context of the local church does not work. Not only does it not work, it hardens people against hearing the call of Jesus in an appropriate setting. "I've already done that," they say. "Nothing happened." Of course it didn't.

A seeker needs to hear the gospel in the environment of a loving fellowship where people really care for each other, encourage each other, show hospitality to each other, etc. just as it says in the New Testament. This is the kingdom of God on earth. Jesus invited people to the Kingdom on earth, not to pie in the sky bye and bye.

In recent years, a few mega-churches have focused their attention on seekers, attempting to bring them to faith by carefully scripted services using drama, art, contemporary music, and "seeker-oriented messages." Many formerly unchurched people have responded. Perhaps the most effective aspect of that approach is that seekers have been exposed to a genuine faith family which exhibits a quality of life not available anywhere else. They witness the joy of Christian fellowship, the concern for needy people in the community, the affection Christians express to each other, the ministries provided by church members, the wisdom of doing things

God's way rather than "the world's way," and they like it. They join. Yes, they trust in Jesus for their eternal salvation, but that salvation is lived out in the context of a healthy and happy faith community.

Now, however, the seeker-driven churches are having problems. They are discovering that Sunday morning church services which concentrate on seekers do not adequately minister to Christians at other levels of spiritual maturity. Those who have moved up the ladder of Christian growth want more "meat" than is offered to seekers: opportunity for significant service, deeper Bible teaching, and the encouragement to radical discipleship. Because the "seeker" services are not meeting their needs, they are moving to other churches.

Does this mean that "seeker-oriented" services don't work? Absolutely not! They work beautifully, for the one purpose they were created: to bring unbelievers to faith. What the present crisis illustrates is the main point of this treatise: no instructional tool can perform more than one function at a time. Every level of spiritual growth requires a different set of tools; those which are appropriate for one level are inadequate for another. Rather than jettison good tools for seekers, churches should consider scrapping the "come-one-come-all" Sunday morning service, or at least use it for a different function.

It also illustrates the need to reexamine the purpose of the Sunday gathering. Is this "service" a weekly re-enactment of a formula, a ritual, a rite, a ceremony, or is it just one tool in the instructional system of making disciples? The New Testament uses three Greek words which are all translated "church:" *ekklesia*, *laos*, and *koinonia*. It is my contention that they are not synonymous, but indicate three separate functions within the life of a local fellowship. *Ekklesia* is the common word for "congregation." It describes the church's corporate persona, distinct from the other institutions of a human community. It is not the Boy Scouts, the city council, or the school board: it is the Christian church. It is that group of 20 to 200 people who have a common identity, who are committed to the same purpose. It is an instructional environment appropriate for teaching, for service projects involving a whole group, and for corporate worship. In situations where the entire membership of the congregation is less than a couple hundred, the *ekklesia* is the whole church; in larger fellowships, Christians find their "*ekklesia* identity" in a Sunday School class, a youth group, a singles fellowship, or a ministry team. They identify themselves by saying, "I'm a member of. . ."

Laos means "people"—in this case, the people of God. *Laos* is much broader than *ekklesia*, and it describes an entirely different aspect of the life of a church. This is the mighty army of God, the church triumphant. When 25,000 men gather in a football stadium for a PromiseKeepers rally, singing "Amazing Grace" with tears streaming down their faces, they are experiencing the power of the *laos*. When a denomination gathers in its national assembly and celebrates the successes of the past year, they are participating in the *laos*. And often, when the congregation of a mega-church joins its thousands of voices in songs of praise, they are feeling the dynamism of the *laos*—the people of God.

The *laos* dimension of the church is also an important instructional tool. This is not the occasion for systematic Bible teaching, for personal nurture in the faith, or for taking care of the routine business of the fellowship. This is the time for celebration, for rallying the faithful to a great cause, for calling to deeper commitment, for proclaiming the greatness of the kingdom of God. By itself, the enthusiasm generated by *laos* moments is quickly dissipated. But combined with the functions of *ekklesia* and *koinonia*, the *laos* element can become the engine which drives a powerful movement of God.

53

Koinonia means "intimate fellowship." The power of small *koinonia* groups has been rediscovered in recent years as the most effective environment for personal growth, recovery from serious afflictions, and behavioral change.

This is where the "one-anothers" of New Testament Christianity take place:

- Instruct one another. (Romans 15:14)
- Agree with one another so that there may be no divisions among you. (I Corinthians 1:10)
- Bear one another's burdens. (Ephesians 4:2)
- Speak to one another with psalms, hymns and spiritual songs. (Ephesians 5:19)
- Admonish one another with all wisdom. (Colossians 3:16)
- Encourage one another. (I Thessalonians 5:11 and Hebrews 3:13)
- Spur one another on toward love and good deeds. (Hebrews 10:24)
- Confess your sins to one another and pray for each other. (James 5:16)

And above all else, love one another. These functions cannot take place in a *laos* gathering; they seldom take place in an *ekklesia* gathering, where all you can see of your friends is the backs of their heads. But they can and will take place in a healthy group of 2-20 people who meet regularly to minister to each other. *Koinonia* intimacy channels the spiritual energy generated by *laos* events and the instruction given in the *ekklesia* into practical application.

Jesus was just as serious about "be(ing) my witnesses" as he was about baptism and observing the communion meal. So why is public testimony not required for church membership, just like baptism and the Lord's Supper? By dropping personal witness from the public gatherings of the church, the most influential tool for the growth of the kingdom has been lost.

I attend several church services every week, but I consider myself a regular member of three fellowships: a mega-church, a mid-sized rural church, and a small denominational church in my neighborhood. In my mega-church, the worship services are carefully-scripted presentations by religious professionals. They are dramatic, polished, awe-inspiring and artistic, but they are not real. They are beautifully-crafted "worship experiences," but they do not showcase real people living out their walk with Christ in everyday life. I haven't heard a "personal witness" there in years. New people are coming every Sunday, but the congregation is not growing numerically.

The mid-sized rural church does better: they have a tradition of encouraging personal "praises" during prayer time and the serving of the Lord's Supper. I look forward to those times. Over the years, the church has seen modest expansion.

My little church has rediscovered one of the roots of their denominational heritage: "personal testimonies." The pastor pre-selects one or two people whom he knows to have something fresh to share: an answer to prayer, the conversion of a family member, physical healing, or something else which demonstrates the power of God in everyday life. Quite often, the "up-front" witness sparks other reports of God's goodness from other members of the congregation. Sometimes, five or six other people will have uplifting stories to relate. The effect is electric: the mature believers are uplifted, the growing Christians are encouraged, and the seekers are allowed to see into the spiritual lives of people who are following Jesus. The church is growing.

If an alcoholic wants deliverance from alcoholism, where does he go? To Alcoholics Anonymous. And what does he hear? Not a treatise on the chemical effects of alcohol on the human body, but personal testimonies of real people who are finding help. If someone wants to lose weight, he goes to Weight Watchers. What do they celebrate every week at Weight Watchers? Real people losing actual pounds. If a person wants to make money outside a regular job, where does that person go? To the rallies of a sales organization or a small-business incubator. And what does he hear? Success stories. And if he goes to the average American church, what does he hear? Everything except the one thing Jesus commanded.

A seeker needs to hear the claims of Christ in the context of a group of people who are demonstrating the benefits of following Jesus. The appeal must be clear, and the evidence must be compelling. If Christians are faithful in following Jesus, there is no need to manufacture evidence. It will happen automatically; all they need is the opportunity to share it.

New Believers

When I was nine or ten, a visiting speaker at our church invited the gathered congregation to make a clear commitment to Christ. "If you want to accept Jesus into your heart and be saved from your sins, come forward and kneel here at the altar." That made sense to me. I had been brought up to believe that this was something I should do, sooner or later, so I left my buddies on the back row and went forward. I prayed with sincerity that God would forgive me and grant me eternal life. I felt good about that.

Then I asked the man who had come to pray with me, "What do I do next?"

"Go back to your seat, keep quiet, and don't cause any more trouble!"

Sad as that may sound, few churches have much more of a clear idea how to handle a new believer. If this is what we are calling people to do, we must have a clear plan, a method or set of methods, appropriate to the person's level of maturity and situation in life, which will enable him or her to take the next steps in spiritual growth.

Most churches have no clue what to do with a new believer. "Enroll him in a class," is the usual response, which translates into: "Teach him the peculiarities of our denomination" or "This is what Presbyterians believe." Going back to school is not what most people had in mind when they made that initial commitment to Christ. They wanted a relationship with God and his people, not a certificate of completion.

Some churches have even less than a class to offer. "Just read your Bible and pray," they say. So this highly motivated novice begins at Genesis 1:1 and is soon bogged down in the "begats" or the dietary restrictions of Leviticus. Finding nothing of substance there, he quits reading. So, he or she sits in church, Sunday after Sunday, settled in at a low level of spiritual growth and maturity.

Jesus taught that entering the kingdom of God is a radical transition. By grace, people are rescued (saved, redeemed, ransomed) from the kingdom of this world and incorporated (adopted, born, translated) into the family of God. To the already-religious Nicodemus, he described this transition as being "born again." To the fishermen who became his disciples, he expressed it in terms of taking up a cross and following him. To every new member of the family of God he prescribed the rite of baptism to signify the transformation that was taking place. Jesus continues to call people to leave the old regime behind and enter the family of God. He entrusts to his disciples the task of issuing out the invitations personally.

Jesus told Simon Peter: "Feed my sheep." (John 21:15-19) This was not only the specific mission assigned to Peter, it was the pattern by which the kingdom was to grow: the big sheep feeding the little sheep. In a normal flock of sheep, shepherds do not feed sheep. Big sheep feed their own babies out of the overflow of their own bodies. In a healthy Christian fellowship, those who are born into the family of God are fed by those who "birthed" them.

Baby lambs are not fed in big groups. They get their nourishment one at a time from a caring mother sheep who gives her baby her undivided attention. Baby Christians cannot be nurtured in big flocks and herds either. They must receive individual attention. In his first letter to the Thessalonians, the Apostle Paul claims that he gave this kind of personal loving attention to every one of the new believers in that fellowship, caring for them like a nursing mother or an encouraging father. (I Thessalonians 2:7-12)

In most churches, the weakest rung of the ladder of spiritual growth is the care of new believers. Yes, curious and interested visitors are coming to church to see what's happening. And, yes, many of those people hear the gospel and respond in faith. Thank God for that. However, the next step in their spiritual growth is so neglected that very few move on to true discipleship. Their growth is stunted because the church is not prepared to nurture them, one by one.

Over the past couple years, I have been watching a wonderful example of how to nurture new believers. One of my neighbors is a successful businessman who has lots of contact with young men who are trying to get established in the same business. They look up to him as a model, although most of them are too full of themselves to admit it. Many of them have grown up in very unhappy and unhealthy family environments and have never known a positive father figure. As far as I know, my neighbor has never made any overt offer to take any of these fellows under his wing and mentor them. He certainly offers no class, no program, and no formal relationship. However, as young men take advantage of his availability, he talks to them out of his own experience, not only about his spiritual life but also about how to conduct business "the right way." I see several of them in church nowadays, taking an active part and apparently enjoying their new life in Christ. That's the way it's supposed to happen: the big sheep birthing lambs, then nurturing them out of the overflow of their own lives until the lambs can feed themselves.

Just like human babies, spiritual newborns must be taught how to talk and how to walk so they can take full advantage of the new world they have been born into. Think about the effort parents put into getting their baby to talk and to take his or her first steps. It requires just as much effort on the part of spiritual parents to get their offspring to talk and walk spiritually. In order to get along in the kingdom, new Christians need to learn how to discuss their spiritual condition with other people, to pray, to give witness to God's blessing, to give thanks, to confess. It's a tedious process to teach a newborn to talk, whether it's a human newborn or a spiritual one, but a loving parent doesn't mind the trouble. In fact, spiritual mothers and fathers delight in it.

Many new believers fail to become disciples because they have gotten the impression that becoming a Christian is a step, like baptism or joining the church or "coming forward." No, the Christian life is a walk: one step after another. The first step is important, because that's when the expectation has to be established that there are many more steps to come. A new Christian has to be taught how to walk in the light, just like a baby has to learn to walk across the living room.

When a boy joins the Cub Scouts, he knows that isn't the end of the process; it's just the beginning. From the very outset, he has the ideal set before him of becoming an Eagle Scout. He knows there is a ladder of achievement and that any boy who commits himself fully can achieve it. The necessary ingredient is faithfulness. Even so in the Christian life.

Growing Christians

The Christian life is not a step (baptism, church membership, confirmation, going forward to the altar), it is a walk—one step after another after another after another. That is how the Apostle Paul described it to the growing Christians at Ephesus:

- Walk about doing good. (Ephesians 2:10 KJV)
- Walk worthy of your calling (Ephesians 4:1 KJV)
- Walk in love (Ephesians 5:2 KJV)
- Walk as children of light (Ephesians 5:8 KJV)
- Walk circumspectly, as wise people, not foolish (Ephesians 5:15 KJV)

I use the King James translation for these verses, since the newer translations substitute "live" for "walk." I understand the rationale for using broadening the meaning of "walk" to include a person's total lifestyle, but I like the symbolism of following Jesus as a walk. He said to his disciples, "Follow me." Being his disciple is a journey, one step at a time, not a ticket to heaven or a reservation for an eternal vacation. It is a daily walk of faith.

Growing Christians need to learn how to walk in the strength and power of the Holy Spirit. They need to learn how to walk in obedience to his Word. They need to know how to walk in humility, not trusting in their own strength, but in God's grace. They need to know how to pray, how to witness to God's faithfulness, how to listen for God's voice, how to apply God's truth to everyday experience. They need to learn the habits of a holy life.

What, then, is the best environment for a growing Christian to learn these spiritual disciplines? The answer to that question depends on the answer to this one: Are spiritual disciplines primarily matter of practice or a matter of cognitive knowledge? Is this a course on swimming or on the history of swimming? One ends in application; the other ends in knowledge. Obviously, the cultivation of holy habits is a practical skill, so it demands appropriate methods for learning skills. This will require a laboratory course, not a lecture. Too much of what we call "Christian education" has been the acquisition of facts rather than the cultivation of habits. We have taught the history and geography of the Holy Land, but not how to apply scripture to life. Our learners can identify Capernaum on the map, but they can't point out pride or deceit lust in their own hearts.

The first lesson in spiritual growth is learning how to pray. That's the one thing the disciples asked Jesus to teach them. I was reared in a godly home, so I assumed I knew how to pray. I did know how to formulate public prayers, but I didn't know how to talk to God.

When I was in college, I was mentored in spiritual disciplines by a fellow from Campus Crusade, to whom I am eternally indebted. He taught me how to pray. The first or second time we met, he said, "You pray."

So I began: "Dear God. . ."

He interrupted me—right when I was praying! "What are doing? Writing a letter or something? Is that how you talk to your roommate when you want his attention: 'Dear Howard'? Start over."

I had never prayed like this, with someone interrupting me and correcting every sentence. But he was teaching me to pray, not to make up prayers.

"I'm not sure what to call God, or which person of the trinity to address," I confessed.

"There are lots of names for God, and many roles which Jesus plays, and several ministries provided by the Holy Spirit. You address God according to your present situation. What do you want to say, or ask, or tell? You address the Father, Son, or Holy Spirit according to the work each one does. When you are sick, who do you go to?"

"To the nurse in the clinic" I said.

"Do you say, 'Dear Nurse, I praise you for all you have done?'"

"No, I say 'I have a splitting headache.'"

"And when you sit in the coffee shop with your girl-friend, do you tell her how sick you are?"

"No, I tell her all the things I like about her and how I feel about her."

"OK, how do you feel about God right now?"

"At this present moment, I feel good about the fact that God is in control of this universe, and I want to be in sync with what he is doing. I think of myself as a soldier reporting for duty, or a worker checking the 'to do' list for the day. I just want to know what he wants me to do today."

"OK," he said, "tell God that."

Every few days, we met and prayed. More precisely, I prayed and he coached me along, until I felt I was communi-cating with God and God was communicating with me.

A growing Christian needs to learn the skill of putting God's truth into practical action. A concise description of this process is found in Paul's letter to young Timothy:

All scripture *is* given by inspiration of God, and *is* profitable for doctrine, for reproof, for correction, for instruction in righteousness: That the man of God may be perfect, throughly furnished unto all good works. (II Timothy 3:16-17 KJV)

This is what I call a philosophy of disciple-making in a nutshell:

- The material of the curriculum: scripture
- The authority: inspired by God
- The methods:
    1. Doctrine: what does it say?
    2. Reproof: what should I change?
    3. Correction: how do I get back on track?
    4. Instruction in righteousness: what positive steps should I take?
- The goal: Christlikeness
    1. Inward maturity
    2 Outwardly equipped for "every good work."

Which mode of the church's program best suits helping growing Christians in their quest for spiritual maturity: *laos*, *ekklesia*, or *koinonia*? The optimal setting for personal growth is *koinonia*—a small group or a one-to-one relationship. Disciples cannot be mass-produced in big flocks or herds. The process requires an intimate, safe, affirming, personal environment. It requires personal accountability for actual behavior—just like swimming. Just because you have read the book doesn't mean you can swim.

Making disciples is a mentoring process that requires a curriculum. "Curriculum" is a good word; it is the Latin word for "racetrack." A racetrack has a starting line, a route, boundaries, and a finish line. Every instructional system has to have a good curriculum. It has to be built around the finish line: what is the desired outcome? Then, where does the learner begin? What are the steps to reach the goal? Are these steps in any order? Are there boundaries?

The finish line for the process of discipleship is Christlikeness—being transformed into the likeness of Christ in character, attitudes, motives, words, and thoughts. Also, it entails doing what Jesus does: healing the sick, doing good, proclaiming the Good News of the kingdom of God, serving others, and so on.

One might ask: "Is this curriculum an individual study or a group project?" The answer is: "Yes."

So, what are the individual lessons in this curriculum? Jesus gave us the course outline when he gave us the first assignment: "Go into all the world and make disciples, baptizing them (setting them apart as a special class) and teaching them to do everything I commanded."

So what did he command?

It doesn't take a rocket scientist to figure that out. I've written a study course based on 36 specific commands of Jesus, but anybody could do the same. Half of those commands fall under the heading "Love God with all your heart, soul, mind, and strength;" the other half under "love your neighbor as yourself."

Remember the test of a good method? Can we do this in Somalia? Absolutely! None of Jesus' commands require buildings, back-lighted screens, websites, or seminary-trained leaders. Can a mentally handicapped person do what Jesus commanded? Absolutely!

The church, that group of believers to which you belong, is the perfect setting for making disciples. God designed it that way. (see Ephesians 4) He brings into every fellowship people with a broad spectrum of spiritual gifts, which if properly employed, provide every aspect of an ideal learning environment. The entire fellowship gives off the pure white light of unity, wisdom, power, and love; but if you examine that light through a prism, you see that it's made up of many colors (gifts) working in harmony. Individual Christians within the Body of Christ operate out of a wide variety of spiritual perspectives (as we will discuss in the section on "Workers"), and together they offer all the resources growing disciples need.

- Those with the gift of teaching clarify the information to be learned
- The care-givers provide emotional support
- Those who are motivated by generosity make resources available
- The prophets point out wrong motives or twisted attitudes
- Those who have gifts of administration organize the whole process
- Encouragers show how to turn problems into projects
- The ones who serve keep the focus on practical ministry.

Working in harmony, as each member makes his or her contribution to the development of the growing disciple, not only the individual, but the whole body matures. The mechanism for this growth is what Paul calls "speaking the truth in love." Each member, coming from the perspective of his unique gift, speaks in love to the others.

Workers

The curriculum for growing Christians is fairly standard: learning to pray, apply scripture, confess sin, give to those in need, walk in the Spirit, etc. The training program for workers is just the opposite: incredibly diverse. According to Romans 12:6, "We have different gifts, according to the grace given us." The same principle is explained in I Corinthians, chapters 7 and 14, and Ephesians, chapter 4. Every person's gift demands a special kind of training. For example, those who are motivated to show compassion require an entirely different set of skills than those who are administrators, prophets, or teachers. The development of their capacities must be tailored to their unique "grace gifts."

The popular church model, which is built on the foundation of pastors doing ministry in a building, is not well-suited for training workers with a wide variety of gifts. Most pastors have been trained in a seminary, not in a church, so they perpetuate the seminary model of training: one instructor delivering conceptual information to passive listeners in 35-minute sound bites, once a week. If that instructional method works for anything, it certainly doesn't equip followers of Jesus to "prepare God's people for works of service." (Ephesians 4:12)

Most American churches operate on a model which has its precedents in business and social organizations—not in scripture: elected officers, committees, majority rule by voting, rotating chairmanship—all according to Roberts' Rules of Order. This formula may work well for the U.S. Congress, but for developing Christian workers, it is dead. It has no usefulness in accomplishing the central tasks of the church.

When I was in seminary, I served a small church which had more positions to fill each year than it had members. So, some people had to report to themselves! The church had accurate minutes of monthly, quarterly, and yearly meetings for more than 100 years, but had dwindled from a large and influential congregation to a mere handful of loyal members. Why did it never occur to anyone to ask, "Is this what Jesus intended? Are we fulfilling our biblical mandate to make disciples and equip them for service with this system?"

The elections-and-offices system has some major instructional deficiencies:

1. Organizational positions seldom reflect spiritual giftedness.
2. Short terms of service do not lend themselves to the life-long development of primary gifts
3. Voting always produces winners and losers, which is totally inconsistent with the spirit of Christian unity.
4. The training appropriate for elected positions (chairman, committee member, board member, superintendent, director, etc.) does not match the kinds of preparation needed for spiritual service. Besides, few churches have any kind of training for its officers.

A congregation needs to hear this constant theme: "We are the body of Christ in this community. We have a job to do. It requires that every member of our fellowship employ the gifts and skills God has given them. And we must coordinate our efforts to do the work of God."

One great resource for today's church is the availability of materials and resources for training workers with specialized gifts: counseling, Bible teaching, youth ministry, small group leadership, stewardship, and so on. The church can be a distribution center for information about seminars, conferences, courses, literature, materials, and support groups for workers-in-training.

In the majority of churches, the only person who receives extensive training is the pastor. To be ordained in most denominations, an aspiring pastor must graduate from a theological seminary of the denomination's choosing. Unfortunately, theological schools cannot provide the kinds of skills a pastor needs to make disciples and equip the saints for ministry. They are stuck with the "Protestant priest" model of ministry, as they have been doing for hundreds of years.

One of the major deficiencies of professional pastoral training is that a seminary is a one-gift outfit. It is not representative of the multi-gifted body of Christ. It is not a real church. The arduous process of graduate school has filtered out those with all the spiritual gifts except teaching, and those teachers are not under the authority of the local church or accountable to it. Consequently, the skills and knowledge offered by theological schools, while intellectually stimulating, have little value to life in the local fellowship. Our evangelical seminaries have been successful in getting their graduates into best graduate schools in the world, but they can't sit down across the table from Sam and talk to him about his walk with God.

A local church needs to be like a university for Christian workers: a core set of basic courses which everyone should take (servanthood, teamwork, planning, biblical principles of service, etc.) and specialized training for the various gift categories (practical service, compassion/care ministries, teaching, stewardship, administration, disciple-building, evangelism, etc.). Some of these training opportunities may be offered on site; others will have to be farmed out to organizations which offer training in specific skills, like counseling, cross-cultural service, and youth ministry. Many denominations already offer these opportunities for their churches; other helps are available through parachurch organizations. The resources are available; all that is needed is the conviction that training workers is a central task of the church, not an add-on. Every member of the Body of Christ must be equipped to deploy his or her gifts in service, first to the Body itself, then to the wider community. Otherwise, it is not a healthy church.

Ministers

A minister is someone who assumes personal responsibility for the spiritual welfare of others. We have been conditioned to think that "ministers" are a professional elite who bear total responsibility for the spiritual health of congregations. No, that is the Roman Catholic understanding of the priesthood. The New Testament teaches that every believer is called to minister. We are all priests.

Jesus' command to "feed my sheep" was not meant for Simon Peter alone. It is the mandate for everyone who says, "You know that I love you," as Simon Peter did. One of the legacies of the Protestant Reformation was "the priesthood of all believers," although it has been affirmed far more than it has been practiced. The biblical model was a multi-gifted fellowship in which every member made a significant contribution to the spiritual development of the whole.

In a healthy church, every growing follower of Jesus must have the opportunity to invest in the lives of others. There should be many formal mechanisms which facilitate this function: Sunday School classes, small groups, youth ministries, outreach teams, Bible studies, hospital visitation programs, jail and prison ministries, mission trips, camps, retreats, and vacation Bible schools—to name a few. In addition to the formal means of ministry, many people in each fellowship should be practicing one-to-one personal disciple-building: meeting friends on a regular basis to encourage them in their spiritual development.

Ministry begins with vision: seeing people as they can be, not simply as they are. Vision is the ability to see the finished product in the raw material, to look at what everybody looks at and see what nobody else sees. Jesus demonstrated this kind of vision when he looked at Simon, a rough Galilean fisherman, and saw Peter, the rock of the church. One who ministers must be able to look at an alcoholic and see a potential saint, to put up with an unruly seventh-grader in the belief that he will become a man of God, to hold a baby in his arms and see the possibility of Christlike development.

Every person's style of ministry is unique. We have differences in temperament, talents, spiritual gifts, experiences, problems we've overcome, and training. No two ministries are alike.

I was speaking to a Sunday School conference about the ministry of Areva Barnes, an 87-year-old grandmother in my church who has raised up many Christian workers through her Sunday School work. (Notice that I didn't say she raised them up in "class." She met them in class, but did most of her training in one-to-one follow-up discussions outside the class.) Areva got off to a poor start: she was married to an alcoholic, divorced, and had two children by the time she was 17. However, she was invited to an evangelical church, heard the gospel, and made a commitment to follow Jesus. Through the years, she invited people to church, took them to dinner in her home, and talked to them about the Lord. For many of those years, her church met in a lawn-mower repair shop. Areva used the formal structures of Sunday School and vacation Bible school to make disciples and equip them for ministry.

"So we should all have a ministry like Mrs. Barnes!" one conference attendee declared.

"No, we shouldn't." I responded. "Each one of us must find his or her own style of ministry. Areva likes to invite people to Sunday School and take them home to dinner and talk about Jesus. That's her method. You have to find your own method. There are lessons we can learn from each other and skills we can pick up from reading about successful ministries, but every one of us must develop a personal style of ministry."

A few nights ago, I was having dinner with some friends, and I asked their three-year-old son Luke what he'd like to be when he grew up. "A cowboy," he said.

"I used to be a cowboy—kind of," I told him.

He was puzzled. "You mean you weren't a real cowboy?"

It was hard for me to explain to a three-year-old the difference between a real cattleman and a hired hand. Yes, I lived on a ranch and took care of cows in exchange for a place to live and a small allowance. However, they were not my cows; they belonged to the owner, Mr. Boring, who was a real cattleman. My job was to feed hay to a couple hundred cows every other day, keep them in the fence, count them, and call Mr. Boring if there were any problems.

Counting two hundred head of range cattle is more difficult than it sounds. I'd get up to "101, 102, 103. . ." then they would all mill around and I'd have to start over. I learned that if I strung the hay out for about a quarter mile, they'd line up in some semblance of a line until I could get a pretty good count.

One day, Mr. Boring came out to check on his cattle. They were all bunched up around the hay wagon, waiting to be fed.

"Where's Gertie?" he asked.

"Who's Gertie? I don't know any Gertie."

"She's that big red Santa Gertrudis. She's not here. She's a tough old range cow, and when she has had a calf, she'll hide it somewhere and stay our there with it rather than coming up to feed. We'd better go look for her; she might be down and need some help."

I was amazed. How could he look at a whole herd of cattle and immediately know not only that a particular one was missing, but why she might be absent. He could identify Gertie's calves from three or four years back and their calves. How did he know that? Because they were his cows and he was their owner.

Jesus made the same distinction between the true shepherd and the hireling. I knew I wasn't a real cattleman; I was a hireling, because I didn't know my cows by name and they didn't know me. I was just the guy who threw hay off the truck, not anyone they knew personally.

Those who are true ministers in a Christian fellowship are shepherds, not hirelings. The Apostle Peter addressed this issue in his letter to younger leaders in the church:

> "To the elders among you, I appeal as a fellow elder, a witness of Christ's sufferings and one who also will share in the glory to be revealed: Be shepherds of God's flock that is under your care, serving as overseers—not because you must, but because you are willing, as God wants you to be; not greedy for money, but eager to serve, not lording it over those entrusted to you, but being examples to the flock. And when the Chief Shepherd appears, you will receive the crown of glory that will never face away."
>
> (I Peter 5:1-4)

One of the reasons some churches fail to make disciples is that their leaders are hirelings, not shepherds. They call themselves "ministers," but they lack the heart of a true shepherd, one who lays down his life for his sheep. They see their job as I saw my role on the ranch: feed them, count them, and keep them in the fence. Their current assignment is just a stepping stone to a more prestigious appointment.

I often ask pastors, "Tell me about your church."

Sometimes I get a response like this: "Well, we're at 167, trying to break the 200 barrier. We're down 10% in Sunday School, but up in other areas. And we're paying all our apportionments, but our building fund is falling behind. If I can keep the numbers up, I might get a call to First Church. . ."

That fellow is a hireling.

On the other hand, ask Dr. Luke about the spiritual retreat at Troas, as recorded in Acts 20. "Yes, Paul was there, accompanied by Sopater from Berea, Aristarchus and Secundus from Thessalonica, Gaius and Timothy from Derbe, and Tychicus and Trophimus from the province of Asia. And a kid named Eutychus, who fell out the window when Paul was preaching." Then Luke goes on through the book of Acts to tell us what happened with these men. He knew them by their names, and he kept track of the progress of their ministries.

Sometimes pastors ask me if I would "help them make disciples." I assume they want me to teach a class or preach a sermon about discipleship. I remind them: "Jesus never talked about the abstract concept of discipleship; he just told us to make disciples. Let's talk about the disciples you're making. Who are the ten most mature men in your church? Where is each one of them spiritually?" Very often, the pastor looks bewildered by such an odd question. He has no idea where his men are spiritually, and he has no way to assess their spiritual health. What's worse is that he has no sense of responsibility that he should be doing that.

"Well, there's Tom. He's been a member for quite a while and is willing to help out if we need any work done around the church."

I keep digging. "Where does Tom work? Have you been to his workplace? How's his home life? Have you spent time with his family in his home?"

One pastor told me: "Those are personal issues. I can't really go there. Besides, it might look like favoritism if I spent more time with one parishioner than another."

So I ask, "Did Jesus go aboard the fishing boats of his disciples on the Sea of Galilee? Did he spend time in their homes? Did he concentrate his time and energy and attention on a few faithful followers? Of course! So, are you smarter than Jesus? Do you have a better method for making disciples than he did?"

Mr. Boring knew more about his cows than many pastors know about the individuals in their congregations. Several times every year, we would "work the cattle." That is, we would round up all two hundred and run them through a chute, one at a time. While their necks were held fast in the chute, Mr. Boring would examine them for ticks, diseases, deficiencies, or injuries. He'd administer pregnancy tests, give them vaccinations, and run them through a tick bath. He'd check their ear tags and write down his observations about them. If pastors, Sunday School teachers, and youth workers want to learn how to make disciples, they should ask a real cattleman or shepherd who knows the importance of accurate assessment and regular check-ups.

The primary instructional need of those disciples who have reached the ministry level of faithfulness is learning how to administer personal, individual spiritual care. According to Ephesians 4:11-16, they should receive this equipping from the apostles, prophets, evangelists, and pastor/teachers who have been assigned to this task by the church. Unfortunately, in the contemporary paradigm of managing congregations, the pastors are so busy managing programs and tending to the needs of strugglers on the lowest levels of the ladder that they have no time to equip a corps of spiritual mothers and fathers to "do the work of the ministry." Consequently, the pastors are exhausted and the churches are weak. A good place to break this cycle of ineffectiveness is to re-define the pastor's role and re-focus his or her efforts on equipping ministers to make disciples rather than building bigger churches. Remember: Jesus promised that if we would make the disciples, he would build the church. Do we believe him?

The new reformation of the church is not a reformation of doctrine, but of ministry. The Protestant Reformation of the 16th century put the Bible back into the hands of the people. The Evangelical Awakening of the 18th century put religion back into the heart. This third reformation is putting the ministry back into the hands of the people.

From the first moments of their spiritual lives, followers of Jesus can minister to others. First, that ministry comes through witness, as the new believer testifies to what God has done in his life. Then, as he gains maturity, he has greater and greater opportunity to invest in the lives of others. The goal is that out of the overflow of his or her own walk with Christ, others' lives will be enriched.

When Jesus commissioned his disciples to "go into all the world and make disciples," they were not very mature spiritually. Matthew 28:17 tells us that "some doubted," even after the resurrection. So why would he entrust the establishment of his kingdom to people who did not have their act together? Partly because he knew they would become mature by building into the lives of other people. We become a disciple by making disciples.

There is a certain threshold of spiritual maturity one cannot cross without getting involved in others' spiritual growth. Followers of Jesus can attain a certain level of growth by studying the Bible, listening to sermons, praying, and attending classes. However, they will not move "up the ladder" of spiritual formation by focusing on themselves. At some point, they must take responsibility for others' growth. As they become channels of grace to others, that same grace will transform their own lives and character.

Equippers

A major shift is underway in ecclesiology—that branch of theology which deals with the nature of the church. The role of congregational leaders is being redefined. In the old "priestly" paradigm, the designated "leaders" (apostles, prophets, evangelists, pastor/teachers) were ordained to carry out the ministry on behalf of the people. Although most would have affirmed the "priesthood of all believers," for all strategic and practical purposes the professional clergy have borne nearly total responsibility for both local churches and networks of churches (denominations).

However, a "cloud as small as a man's hand began rising above the sea" (I Kings 18:44) of the ministerial monopoly. The first shaking of the foundations began with the discovery that "the comma does not belong in Ephesians 4:11." That is, the role of these individuals with exceptional gifts was not to perform the ministry, but to equip the saints to do the work of the ministry. A group of missionaries to India who were on a spiritual retreat in the early 1950s rediscovered the works of Roland Allen. They read Allen's books, The Spontaneous Expansion of the Church and Missionary Methods; St. Paul's or Ours, and the "equipping church" movement was born. Allen's work had been forgotten for decades, but the discovery of his writings ushered in a whole new understanding of the role of ministers. Time will tell whether the "equipping movement" will be a sea change in the understanding of the pastorate or merely an alternative perspective. Either way, those who attain or are promoted to these levels of authority need new tools to equip the entire church for service.

The other significant influence on the shape of Christian ministry came from John Greenleaf's book Servant Leadership. Written originally for board members of charitable organizations, Greenleaf reminded churchmen what Jesus had said about servanthood (Matthew 20:25-28). "Ah, yes," some rulers of congregations recalled, "we're supposed to be servants of these people, not masters." Seminaries renamed their standard courses to reflect their new-found emphasis on servant leadership: "Preaching as Servant Leadership," "The Theology of Servanthood," and so on. It remains to be seen whether the rediscovery of servanthood will transform pastoral ministry or be replaced by the next new theme.

There is considerable debate these days about the role of apostles and prophets. On one hand are those who believe the Bible itself has replaced the need for apostles and prophets. Others, especially in Africa, arrogate the title "Apostle" or "Prophet" to themselves and have those titles printed on their business cards. I will avoid that debate and focus instead on the one role which is pre-eminent in every congregation: the pastor/teacher.

Teachers play a key role in the life of the church. Their job is to interpret the teachings of Jesus and equip the congregation to apply his principles to everyday life. Jesus himself was recognized as "a teacher sent from God." (John 3:2) His followers called him "Teacher." His role, as he described it to Pontius Pilate, was "to bear witness to the truth." (John 18:27) He not only taught the Word of God, he was the Word made flesh. And, he promised that when he was no longer physically with us, his Spirit would continue to lead us into all truth. (John 16:13)

The highest calling of Christian discipleship is to be a witness to the truth, a teacher of Jesus' message. In a certain sense, every follower of Jesus bears this responsibility. In a special sense, some disciples rise to the level of teachers to the whole congregation. In Ephesians 4:11, they are called "pastor/teachers" or "shepherds who teach." These are not priests who carry out sacerdotal duties on behalf of the congregation; they are members of the fellowship who assume the responsibility to guard and proclaim the Word of the Lord. This is an important distinction.

The Apostle James said there should not be many teachers, and that they are held to strict standards of accountability. (James 3:1) The Apostle Paul defined his role as "as teacher of the true faith to the Gentiles." (I Timothy 2:7, II Timothy 1:11) Those whom God raises up to bear this mantle of "teacher" stand in the great tradition of prophets and spiritual instructors like Ezra who "devoted himself to the study and observance of the Law of the Lord, and to teaching its decrees and laws in Israel. (Ezra 7:10)

The great need today is the training of pastor/teachers, not to perform the ministry of the church as in the old "priestly paradigm," but to equip the believers for ministry. The old tools are no longer adequate, since the industry they supported is obsolete. The new understanding of the church, if it takes hold, will demand an entirely new set of models, methods, and assessment tools.

The Community

I am a member of several layers of community: my neighborhood (Columbus Harbour), my city (Longwood), my metropolitan area (Orlando), my state (Florida), my country (the U.S.A.), and the world. I have responsibilities at every level of that pool of humanity as well as the environment in which they live. I have duties as a citizen, a neighbor, and a friend.

Mine is a mixed community: believers, non-believers, and anti-believers. Some share most of my values; some share none. Whoever they are, I must do my part to contribute to their well-being, their safety, and their freedom.

Unlike some of my Christian colleagues, I do not believe that my service to the community is "pre-evangelism." I owe my neighbors my respect and my participation in community activities, regardless of their spiritual disposition. If, in the process, they notice that I am a follower of Jesus and want to know more about him, that's fine, but it is not an issue regarding my community service.

Others of my Christian friends feel that community transformation should be our primary objective: restoring neighborhoods in the name of Jesus. No, I don't believe that either. Jesus didn't transform Nazareth, Capernaum, or Jerusalem, nor did he command his disciples to do so. I have never witnessed a community which has been "developed" by Christians, despite the fact that many have tried. I do know we are to be light, salt, and leaven in the world in which we live. I know we are to care for the poor, feed the hungry, work toward freedom for the oppressed, and promote justice, whether next door or in Afghanistan. But I do not expect any of those communities to be "Christianized," totally transformed by my efforts or those of fellow Christians.

I serve my community for an entirely different reason than I make disciples. I have an obligation to help a seeker to become a believer or a believer to become a disciple because of who <u>he</u> is: a person who is faithful to Jesus at some level. I have an obligation to serve my community because of who <u>I</u> am: a follower of Jesus. That's what Jesus' people do: serve others. That's what Jesus did. He healed the sick and responded with compassion to the needs of people he met, regardless of their spiritual commitment. He did not say, "I will heal you if you will follow me." He just healed them.

I bought a book with the intriguing title <u>Conspiracy of Kindness</u>—simply because I liked the title. I thought, "This is what Christians should be doing: scheming together how to show kindness to people." However, when I got into the book, I discovered that the acts of kindness they were advocating were thinly-guised advertisements for their local church. "We'll wrap your Christmas presents for you, and here's the address of our church." No, Jesus didn't do that.

Jesus showed compassion for people because of who he was: the Son of a loving God. We, too, reflect the character of our Heavenly Father, who has sent us into the world to do good. If the recipients of our kindness "give glory to our Father in heaven," that is a bonus. If they don't, that's OK. We seek our approval only from the One who sent us into the world as his ambassadors, whether or not or service is appreciated by them.

Conclusion

Jesus said, "<u>You</u> make disciples. . .<u>I</u> will build my church, and the gates of Hades will not overcome it." (Matthew 20:19-20 and Matthew 16:18) The modern church has responded, "Thank you, Jesus, but we have a better plan: we will build our churches, and you may make disciples in them, if you wish." Consequently, we have your church, my church, and their church, and in most places the gates of Hades are doing fine. Of course, no one blatantly announces, "Jesus, we are leaving the task of making disciples to you," but that is the underlying assumption. If disciples are to be made at all, it is his responsibility, not the primary task of the assembled believers. I often ask congregations, "Who is in charge of your Sunday School?" They can name the person. "And who is in charge of preparing the elements for communion?" Again, the identity of the communion steward is public knowledge. "And who is responsible for making disciples?" I always get a blank stare, because no one has been assigned that task. Consequently, very little disciple-making gets done.

The church is suffering a crisis of belief. We really don't believe that if we do what Jesus told us to do, he will do what he promised to do. We believe in him enough to save us from our sins, but not enough to obey his basic commands: to witness, to love one another, and to make disciples.

God is raising up a new generation of workers from many nations of the world who share the core beliefs of a new reformation:

1. That God's ultimate intention is that every believer come to full maturity in Christ.
2. That making disciples is the foundation to every other ministry: evangelism, social justice, caring for the poor, serving the church.
3. That the basic curriculum for discipleship is obeying the commands of Jesus.
4. That the role of pastor/teachers is to equip the saints for the work of the ministry, not to do the ministry themselves.
5. That the local church should be an instructional system for making disciples, with appropriate tools designed for people at every level of spiritual growth and service.
6. That we bring glory to God by bearing fruit—the fruit of the Spirit expressed in Christlike character, and the multiplication of disciples through intentional investment in individual lives.